KEVIN BALESTRIERI

HOME
TEAM

Four Easy Ways to Communicate with Your
Contractor, Architect, and Designer to
Get the Results You Want

ENDORSEMENTS

In my 35-plus years as an architect and design professional, I have learned that the most important aspect of all successful projects is clear and open communication.

I applaud Kevin for writing this book and helping the average person understand how to get the most out of the building process and see their dreams realized.

Carl E Campos
Architect, CEO
LCA Architects

Home Team is an easy-to-read and understand guide for homeowners contemplating a remodel or renovation project. Kevin Balestrieri presents a brief, but concise, roadmap with his four-step process for assisting homeowners with understanding and communicating clearly with their "Home Team" design and construction professionals. A must-read for homeowners to help ensure a successful project.

Thomas Beckett
Design, Construction, and Project Management
Consultant
President, tBP Architecture

HOME TEAM

Four Easy Ways to Communicate with Your Contractor, Architect
and Designer to Get the Results You Want

Kevin Balestrieri
Copyright© 2012

ISBN-13: 978-0615903446
ISBN-10: 0615903444

BALI Publishing

Printed in the United States of America

TABLE OF CONTENTS

DEDICATION

To my mom and dad, for always providing me with the influence that "hard work always pays off."

To my mom, who always stood up for me when my teachers didn't think I should be learning with all the other kids when I was growing up.

To my dad, for always showing me that family is your #1 asset in life.

To my two older brothers, Scott and Todd, for always taking me under their wing in life and business and letting me know that no matter what I do, they will always be there for me. Individually, I thank Scott for teaching me that "your word and relationship" is the most important aspect in business, and Todd, for showing me the ins and outs of how to run a company.

To Ann Fryer, (Learning Disability) counselor at Cal Poly, for always understanding the way I would learn.

To my coach, Payam Saadat, for coaching me at Cal Poly and teaching me the importance of hard work and dedication on and off the field.

To all my football teammates at Cal Poly San Luis Obispo, for teaching me what TEAMWORK is all about.

All these people have contributed to my life in one way or another. They have taught and shown me love, compassion, hard work, dedication, and perseverance. I can't thank you enough for helping me write *Home Team*.

FOREWORD

Every building project is, in essence, a prototype.

When a computer or automobile maker designs a new product, the team of designers, engineers, and fabricators works together to make the "first" of many. Bugs and difficulties are worked out as the prototype moves toward production.

In the construction industry, we don't have that luxury—our product has to work right the first time! Kevin Balestrieri explains how this minor miracle can happen and why the right team is everything.

Home Team explains, better than any book I've read, how a home gets conceived and built, all in accessible, no-nonsense language. I will be providing all of my clients with a copy.

Mark English, AIA San Francisco
Architectural poster child for Houzz.com

CHAPTER 1

INTRODUCTION

If you're like most homeowners, you've probably already heard from friends and neighbors that a remodel or renovation can be a time-consuming and challenging chain of events—which never goes according to plan—and is expensive, too!

My name is Kevin Balestrieri, and I wrote this book to teach homeowners the best way to get what they want out of a home remodel or renovation.

I have been in the construction industry for more than eighteen years. I received my undergraduate degree in Business Communication from California Polytechnic State University, San Luis Obispo, followed by a certificate in Construction Management from Hayward State University. I am also a licensed general contractor, specializing in high-end residential construction, as well as commercial construction.

My company, Bali Construction, does over 100 projects each year. I work with homeowners just about every day—and I see some of the same issues develop over and over again. Why? Because as a general contractor, I know the ins and outs of running a construction project. Homeowners don't, and they need to do their research before they start any kind of construction process. These disconnects can be on the challenging side, both for me and for the homeowner.

Don't get me wrong. I like to be challenged in life, but some of these situations could be avoided completely if homeowners knew just a little bit more about what I know!

This book is intended to help homeowners:

- understand what happens in a construction project

- learn what works and what doesn't

- get past the notion that every contractor is out to get them

- learn to trust their HOME TEAM

- Overcome their fears about starting a construction project

Most of all, I want to show you how exciting it is to build your dream home!

I'll explain the construction process and help you work with your renovation team to get the beautiful house you want, without the usual home-induced headaches. Most important, with this book, you will understand the importance of teamwork in a home project. When everyone is on the same page, working together, the result is a great finished product and a happy homeowner.

CHAPTER 2

THE LAY OF THE LAND

Before we dive in on to how to improve your experience when you renovate your home, let's get our feet wet by going through a basic renovation, from idea to completion, together. The building professionals you ultimately choose will have gone through this many times, but unless you have a contractor in the family, you're probably not familiar with the process.

You might ask if the process is any different from when you drop your car off to have the brakes replaced. *It's not like I would need to learn anything about being a mechanic*, you might be thinking. Keep in mind that knowing the steps of a home renovation is half the battle. What you'll learn in this chapter will help you "talk the talk" as you interview your team—but more on that a bit later.

First, let's get a reading on the people who will be helping you make your dream-home a reality.

Who's Who

Most construction teams consist of an architect, a designer, a general contractor, and a structural engineer.

Role	What They Do for You
An **architect** is a licensed professional who designs buildings and may also supervise their construction. While requirements vary from region to region, an architect's license is conferred only upon those with appropriate education and experience, who subsequently pass a state-mandated examination.	The architect puts the plan together, draws it out on paper, and works very closely with the owner on how they want everything laid out.
A **designer** specializes in planning the interior, including surfaces, fixtures, and furnishings, of an architectural space. While a variety of certifications are available to designers, licenses are not required. However, a designer usually completes a two- or four-year educational program prior to certification by one of the industry bodies.	A designer works very closely with the homeowner to choose all the finishes, the interior elements: the cabinets, the countertops, the flooring, the trim detail, the window detail, and also the color scheme.

Role	What They Do for You
A **structural engineer** is a licensed professional engineer who reviews and analyzes architectural plans in order to ensure safety and make sure design goals are achievable. Structural engineers may also make recommendations to improve efficiency in construction and to enhance the comfort of occupants. A structural engineering license is conferred only upon those with appropriate education and experience, who subsequently pass both a national and a state examination.	A structural engineer runs calculations against the architect's plan to ensure, for example, that you can physically build a third story on your house.
A **general contractor** is a licensed member of the building trades, who is responsible for the construction, improvement, repair, or demolition of a building, under contract to the building's owner. The general contractor is responsible for the overall job.	A general contractor actually builds the project, as planned by the architect and the designer.

Role	What They Do for You
In California, a general contractor's license is conferred only upon those with at least four years of experience or education in the trade for which they are licensed. (They must also be fingerprinted, have an FBI background check, and be bonded!)	

The Construction Process

Let's begin with something small (well, smaller than a full build or full remodel, anyway). Let's say our homeowner, Jane, wants to completely remodel her bathroom. She'll probably start by asking her friends, neighbors, and co-workers for recommendations for a general contractor or an architect.

TEAM TIP

My recommendation is to call an architect from the get-go. Because we want our example to proceed smoothly, we'll go with an architect. As you read through the process, see if you can guess why!

Jane sets out to do her homework as she chooses an architect. She checks her friends' and Yelp's recommendations. She looks at the architects' websites to see what types of work they've done.

TEAM TIP

Make sure the architect has done work similar to the work you want done—if they've only worked on schools or restaurants, they are probably not the best choice for your bathroom renovation.

Jane selects a few architects whose past work appeals to her. She interviews them, and they ask about her design wants and wishes, her inspiration for the project, and also about her budget. When she narrows it down to one or two architects, they come to Jane's house, and as part of the proposal process, they measure the existing bathroom to ensure the planned design will fit the space.

Now, the architect will get additional information from the city, to make sure the project Jane wants is within the bounds of existing zoning and other laws. (For example, if Jane's house was a recognized historic building, she might not be able to change anything at all!)

From there, the architect will generate a plan of the existing structure, which will be needed if he is selected for the project. There is a reason for this. In order to get a permit from the city, he will need to show an *existing plan*—the way the house is now—and, eventually, a *proposed plan*, which shows the way the house will look once all the work is done.

But in the meantime, based on the existing plan, Jane's architect candidates will hand-draw new, proposed areas, and show their proposals to Jane. The architect may also make an estimated budget for the project.

At this point in the process, Jane must decide which of the architects she's been working with is the one who will be selected for the project, and appropriate contracts would be signed.

(Now in this simplified example, we're going to say that the architect on this project is also going to serve as the designer ... and at this stage in the process, the architect/designer and the homeowner will begin to nail down the design path. In other words, does Jane want a modern look? Traditional? Does she want to re-create Elvis's bathroom in her own home?

The architect (who, remember, is also Jane's designer) puts together a rough plan, which is then given to a structural engineer. The structural engineer will review the plan to make sure the project can physically be built, according to engineering best practices.

(You might be asking yourself how Jane found that structural engineer ... in some cases, the homeowner contracts with and pays the structural engineer for services, while in other cases, the structural engineering review is simply a line-item on the architect's invoice.)

Once the plans are blessed by the structural engineer, the architect brings in a general contractor, who will put together preliminary budgeting and a rough schedule, and those reports are presented to our homeowner, Jane. (Of course, she might not approve the preliminary plans immediately. The budget, the schedule, or even the design itself may need further refinement, but since we're going through a simple example, let's assume everything looks perfect on the first go.)

A sample bid proposal is shown below.

BALI
BUILDING A STRONG FUTURE

General Requirements	Contract Amount	Revisions to Date	Comment/Notes
Subtotal - General Requirements	$0.00		
Site Work Construction		Revisions to Date	Comment/Notes
Subtotal - Site Work Construction Division	$0.00		
Concrete Division		Revisions to Date	Comment/Notes
Subtotal - Concrete Division	$0.00		
Masonry Division		Revisions to Date	Comment/Notes
Subtotal - Masonry Division	$0.00		
Metals Division		Revisions to Date	Comment/Notes
Subtotal - Metals Division	$0.00		
Woods & Plastics Division		Revisions to Date	Comment/Notes
Subtotal - Woods & Plastics Division	$0.00		
Thermal & Moisture Protect		Revisions to Date	Comment/Notes
Subtotal - Thermal & Moisture Protect	$0.00		
Doors & Windows Division		Revisions to Date	Comment/Notes
Subtotal - Doors & Windows Division	$0.00		
Finishes Division		Revisions to Date	Comment/Notes
Subtotal - Finishes Division	$0.00		
Specialties Division		Revisions to Date	Comment/Notes
Subtotal - Specialties Division	$0.00		
Equipment Division		Revisions to Date	Comment/Notes
Subtotal - Equipment Division	$0.00		
Furnishings Division		Revisions to Date	Comment/Notes
Subtotal - Furnishings Division	$0.00		
Special Construction Division		Revisions to Date	Comment/Notes
Subtotal - Special Construction Division	$0.00		
Conveying Systems Division		Revisions to Date	Comment/Notes
Subtotal - Conveying Systems Division	$0.00		
Mechanical Division		Revisions to Date	Comment/Notes
Subtotal - Mechanical Division	$0.00		
Electrical Division		Revisions to Date	Comment/Notes
Subtotal - Electrical Division	$0.00		
Pre & Post Construction		Revisions to Date	Comment/Notes
Subtotal - Pre & Post Construction Division	$0.00		
Sub-Total all Divisions	$0.00		
Insurance 0%	$0.00		
Contractor's Fee 0%	$0.00		
GRAND TOTAL	$0.00		

Once the preliminary plan is accepted by the homeowner, the architect must go to the city and get what is known as a plan-check from the planning department. Once the plan-check is complete, the general contractor generates a more detailed version of the plan, sometimes containing multiple pricing variations.

TEAM TIP

At this point in the process, some homeowners prefer to get bids from multiple general contractors, which can help ensure that the project budget is reasonable for the work proposed. Keep in mind that the lowest bid may not necessarily represent the best finished product—more on this later.

So let's review the process: Jane has settled on a general contractor, and she and the contractor sign ... a contract!

Now that the project is officially a "go," the general contractor puts together a proposed schedule for the project, and the architect submits final plans to the city planning department. If the city's criteria are met, permits are issued.

Here's an example of a proposed schedule. (The right side of the page is a graphical version of the schedule, showing progress bars for every line item.) Look down the columns at the left side of the page; this is a list of all major tasks that will need to be checked off before the job is considered complete. (We'll discuss check-off in greater detail later.)

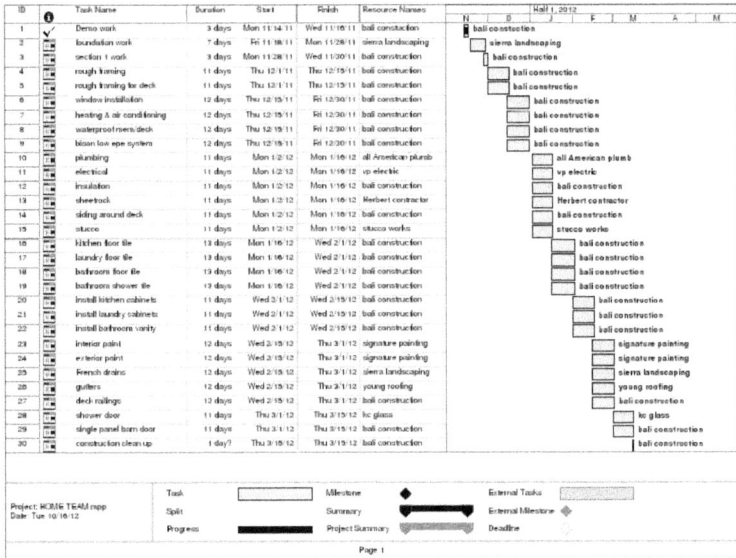

Did you know? California state law says that a down payment may not exceed $1,000.00 or 10% of the contract price, whichever is less.

Once permits are issued, the work can start—and that means your team needs to be paid. Remember that up to this point, your general contractor has not been paid! Generally, the contractor asks for a deposit, and once that is paid, the work can start.

Note that if work begins before a permit is issued, the homeowner may be fined!

During this period, Jane should be getting regular status and schedule updates from the general contractor, and she will also be notified promptly if any unexpected issues arise.

Jane's general contractor will also inform her, well in advance, of any upcoming milestones that are part of the schedule. For example, new bathroom fixtures may need to be ordered by a certain date to make sure they will be delivered on time, ensuring the project remains on schedule.

The contractor will also be required to undergo periodic city inspections from time to time. In most cases, these inspections are tied to progress payments that are specified in the contract. These inspections help Jane know that work is being performed appropriately and on schedule.

Then, finally, all the work is done! The general contractor puts together a manual describing everything that was purchased, such as fixtures and materials, all the permit paperwork, budgets versus costs, the proposal for the project, photographs of the project that were taken, sometimes daily, to show progress, and this entire book is presented to Jane. At that time, the GC's final payment, in many cases, a 5% holdback) is due.

What's left to do? Before Jane can run off to enjoy her gorgeous, new bathroom, she must file a *notice of completion*. This legal document indicates the project has been completed per the architectural specifications and that the work was performed to the satisfaction of the homeowner.

Design/Build Process Review

Here's a handy checklist shared by my colleague, Craig O'Connell, containing all the project steps your architect is likely to do. You may find it handy to refer to, no matter where you are in the process!

1. Measure the job site.

2. Get client's wish list: images, requirements, initial design information.

3. Check with city for any zoning, setback, or other potential issues.

4. Create base model of plans (the existing layout).

5. Create hand drawings of proposed floor plan.

6. Work with homeowner to choose a design.

7. Develop construction documents.

8. Provide design documents to structural engineer, if needed.

9. Select fixtures and finishes, keeping an eye on lead time.

10. Homeowner gives final approval of fixtures, finishes, etc.

11. Generate additional architectural drawings (also called the "full set"). These are used for final pricing with the general contractor.

12. Once the permit is issued, construction begins.

13. Architect performs site visits to keep design intent in place and assists, as needed, to keep the project moving along.

Architect's Corner

Whew! That's an example of the happy path ... but we've all heard the horror stories. To better understand why things can go wrong, we asked architect Tommy Pippin, A.I.A., about his take on the pitfalls of home renovation projects. His advice: the key elements to creating a successful construction project are:

- understanding expectations,

- understanding the division of labor,

- checks and balances, and

- communication.

Understanding Expectations. Knowing what the homeowner expects helps everyone stay on the same page. Obviously, the architect needs to understand what the homeowner wants the finished project to look like, but the expectations can be elaborated upon for the contractor. For instance, Pippin asks clients, "Will someone be on site full-time? What can we expect when an issue is discovered? What is the routing of communications? How often does the homeowner need to see the project and check in?"

Division of Labor. Establishing divisions of labor at the beginning of a project helps keep everyone in sync. Pippin routinely asks his clients, "Does the owner expect the contractor to keep the plants that are on site alive during construction? Does the contractor expect the owner to provide power to the site? Does the homeowner expect the designer to provide the decorative light fixtures? Does the homeowner expect the contractor to install owner-purchased appliances?"

Checks and Balances. Everything moves more smoothly when the homeowner knows how the overall building process works. At every stage in the process—from initial drawings to contractor selection, from pricing to contract, and so on to the final punch list—it's mission-critical for the team to check each other's work. But you can't leave the homeowner out of the picture and then expect him to be thrilled with the end result: the homeowner needs to be involved along the way. According to Pippin, "Informing the homeowner along the way when they are expected to review is a key element."

Communication. Sometimes, there can be a lack of communication between an architect and general contractor. I've found through experience that this occurs when I'm not hired for contract administration. The general contractor is simply left to his own best judgment and consequently takes on additional liability through no fault of his own. Pippin's recommendation:

> At minimum, a homeowner should have the architect make weekly site visits. It ... allows the architect to double-check for any issues the contractor may have not seen. It's always in the homeowner's best interest to have more eyes on potential problems and opportunities for improvement.

As with so many other situations, communication can spell the difference between success and failure on a home renovation project. The following chapters show you what you need to know to ensure success—and a beautiful home!

The Four Cs

To this end, we have developed a four-step process to help homeowners communicate clearly with their home-improvement team—their Home Team—and ensure successful completion of their projects. The tools are:

- Connect
- Communicate
- Check-Off, and
- Completion

CHAPTER 3

CONNECT

If you've read the previous chapter, you now have a good understanding of how home renovation projects come together.

So what's next? You need to do a little pre-work to refine your project concept, and then you need to find a set of professionals who can bring your dreams to reality. On their own, either of these tasks could seem daunting, but the better your connection, both to your own wants and also to prospective team members, the more smoothly your project will run, once it's underway.

How do you make those connections? **Connect** means:

- *Homework.* The homeowner has done her homework and knows what she wants.

- *Research.* The homeowner has researched prospective home team members.

- *Making connections.* The homeowner seeks to make connections during team member interviews.

We'll dive in and find out more below.

Homework

Everyone hates homework, but we promise, this kind of homework can actually be fun.

Before you call that first architect, before you ask your friends for contractor recommendations, *you need to have a solid idea of what you want.*

It's easy to see the benefits of doing your homework: first of all, if you want a sleek, modern kitchen, full of high-end, commercial appliances that would make Gordon Ramsay jealous, then a recommendation for the guy who built out your neighbor's brother's rustic farmhouse kitchen may not help you that much.

And second, if you don't know what you want, it's going to be nearly impossible for you to effectively communicate your desires to an industry professional.

So go through those house-beautiful magazines. Watch the DIY channel on television to help you narrow down what you like, and also, what you don't. Learn what you can live with and what you can't live without.

Keep a folder with clips you've torn out of magazines and images you've printed from the Internet. This will help you see patterns in your own choices. For example, you might always go for the room with the checkerboard floor, or every bedroom you choose has robin's-egg blue walls. That folder will also come in handy later: when you start to talk with architects, designers, and contractors, a picture truly is worth a thousand words.

Sites like houzz.com can be a real resource during this phase of the project. In fact, I like houzz.com so much that I set my clients up with an account and walk them through the choices and options. It seems to really help them pick out ideas and drill down to what they truly want.

Once you have your likes and dislikes firmly in mind, the next step is to ask around for recommendations. In addition to your friends, neighbors, and co-workers, you'll also want do a little discovery yourself. The Yellow

Pages®, Yelp®, and Google® are great sites to help you create a list of potential home construction professionals. Once you have your list, you can move on to the next step: research.

Research

Though it can sound complicated, researching your team is fairly straightforward. Let's talk about what to look for when doing your research.

Begin your research by taking a look at an architect's or contractor's website. Look at how long they've been in business and at the photographs on their site. Does their site demonstrate considerable experience?

If they have a gallery of past jobs, compare the types of jobs they show you with the pictures you clipped as you were doing your homework. Does your style match, or fit, with theirs?

Look at the testimonials, and review what past clients say. There should be no red flags here, because a contractor is not going to include a negative testimonial on his own website, but taken overall, what do clients say about the contractor's punctuality, communication style, and work ethic?

As you go, weed out any professionals whose style or experience isn't a good fit with your wishes. If you're interested in a Craftsman-style finished product, then interviewing architects/designers who specialize in the modern look is probably not going to bring you what you wanted.

Once you've narrowed it down to a handful of people on your "short call" list, check each person to ensure they have appropriate licenses and insurance. In most states, you can verify license status for home professionals at the department of consumer affairs.

In California, you can refer to http://www.cab.ca.gov/consumers/license_verification.shtml for architects and https://www2.cslb.ca.gov/OnlineServices/CheckLicenseII/CheckLicense.aspx for contractors.

Verify that the contractor is not only licensed, but is licensed to work on the type of project you have in mind.

Insurance

You also need to verify that your architect, designer, or contractor maintains appropriate general liability insurance. Contractors who have employees should also carry workers' compensation insurance. Note that, in California, the amount of workers' compensation insurance contractors need to carry is based on the total business they have done during the preceding year.

This type of insurance is so important, because if you hire someone who is uninsured or underinsured and they (or an employee of theirs) are subsequently injured while on your property, you, the homeowner, are legally responsible.

In addition, if the general contractor has employees, the contractor must have workers' compensation insurance. They should also carry general liability insurance, and in California, contractors must be bonded.

Keep in mind that required insurance levels are based upon the amount of business the contractor does: the more projects worked, the more liability the contractor has. So having a large amount of insurance doesn't mean the contractor has risky business practices. The more business he does, the more insurance he is required to have.

You can usually verify an architect or contractor's insurance status through your state's consumer affairs website.

Subcontractors

Now a word about subcontractors: a general contractor may have employees, or he may hire out certain jobs—for example, pouring concrete, or rigging electrical wiring—to qualified subcontractors. The employee-versus-sub-contractor balance varies from company to company.

You need to ask your prospective contractor for a list of all employees and a list of all subcontractors they plan to use on your job. The contractor should be happy to provide this to you. With that list, you will want to verify that the subcontractors have appropriate workers' compensation and general liability insurance, and are bonded, just as you did for the general contractor.

Reviews and Complaints

As you do your research, you may see complaints (on review sites like Yelp or on the state's consumer affairs website) about a home professional.

A short note about review sites: Internet reviews are usually best taken with a grain of salt. A terrific contractor may have only one or two reviews out there, especially if he doesn't request them from clients at the end of every job. Keep in mind that a bad review can happen to anyone. Of course, if you find a number of negative reviews, especially distributed over a period of time, that's definitely a red flag.

A complaint recorded by the state licensing board should obviously be taken more seriously. The homeowner can ask what the complaint was, what happened, and why there was a complaint, and then call additional references to determine if it could have been a fluke.

Next Steps

Once you've vetted your short list, it's time to set up screening calls, and then interviews.

Making Connections

The first question, as you get ready to set up interviews, is to figure out if your planned job is big enough to need an architect. Any job that is more than just cosmetic (if you're doing anything beyond changing the fixtures), will benefit from the wisdom and experience of an architect. If you're really unsure, a call to your city's planning department can usually help you figure it out.

If you're going to be using an architect, you'll want to start with those screening calls first. Working from the short list you developed as you did your homework and research, contact the architects and tell them how you found them. Let them know the type of project you are interested in doing. Talk about styles and try to find out what they are passionate about as far as design. (Hint: the answer here should not be "everything.") Ask the architect what his preferred process is.

TEAM TIP

What would happen if you called a general contractor first? Well, one of the first questions they will ask you, if your project is of a certain size and complexity, is "Who is your architect?" The general contractors you speak with may want to have an architect involved before getting into specifics about schedule or budget. Let your general contractor guide you in determining whether or not an architect should be involved; if your contractor says you need an architect, listen to his advice!

If you do end up speaking to general contractors before you begin working with an architect, make sure to ask about the contractor's qualifications that are specific to the project you want to do. If they've renovated hundreds of kitchens but never an entire house, they may not be a great fit for your needs.

Listening

Once you've shared your wants and desires for the project, ask about their experience with that kind of project—and *listen to the response*!

That may sound silly ("Of course I'm going to listen!" you're saying right now), but it's harder than you might think. Because you're in the process of hiring a team, your natural inclination is to ask a lot of questions, control the conversation, and be in the driver's seat. As much as you can, try to resist that impulse. In this stage of the process, you can learn a tremendous amount about the person's communication style—if you're prepared to listen.

Ask open-ended questions, and as you hear the answers, check for the following:

- Are they asking you intelligent, applicable questions?

- Do they listen to you?

- Are they working with you, or do they have their own, set agenda?

- If, for whatever reason, they can't give you the design you want, are they adept at providing you with options?

- Do they seem genuinely interested in you, or is this just a job to them?

- Does this person seem very organized?

- Does this person have the patience to answer every one of your questions, no matter insignificant they might be?

- Is the person able to demonstrate that they understand what you want?

Questions to Ask Architects and Designers

- How long have you been in business?

- How do you generally approach a project?

- How will you approach this project?

- What architectural styles are you passionate about?

- What is your fee structure?

- Will you be handling my job personally? Who else is on your team?

- Which contractors do you usually work with?

- What is your experience working in this particular county or city?

- What is your familiarity with the local planning process?

- Do you have references/referrals?

Questions to Ask General Contractors

- Are you licensed? How long have you been licensed?

- How long have you been in the construction business?

- How big is your crew? Are they employees or subcontractors?

- Will you, personally, be on the job site every day?

- Who is responsible for getting permits?

- How long do you estimate the project will take?

- What is the best way to get in contact with you? What is your usual response time to phone messages or e-mails?

- What professional organizations are you a member of?

- Will you provide lien waivers for subcontractors?

- When do you think you could start on my project?

- How many projects will you be running concurrently?

- How many projects similar to mine have you completed in the last year?

- Which architects do you usually work with?

- Ask about license and insurance (even though you've done your homework and know the answer). Make sure that what the contractor tells you matches up with what you've already learned.

- What kinds of services do you offer before, during, and after the completion of the project?

- How will you handle common issues that arise during construction?

- What is your experience working in this particular county or city?

- What is your familiarity with the local planning process?

- Do you have references/referrals?

- Do you guarantee your work?

Trust

As you conduct the interview, ask yourself if you're finding anything in common with the person you're speaking to.

Wait a minute, you may be thinking as you read this. *We're not going on a date; I just want someone to fix my bathroom.*

Yes, that's very true, and you're right. It's not about dating, not at all, but these little connections are what help you learn more about the other person, and they will help you *build trust.*

That trust is key to a successful outcome on your project.

You're going to be trusting the people you choose with entry to your home, with the care and construction of one of your biggest assets (for most people, THE biggest asset), and you need to trust their knowledge and expertise about the best way to complete the job for you.

Of course, trust isn't built right away. So give it a little time, but if you're not feeling a connection in those initial conversations, that should tell you something, too. Trust your gut instincts.

Because no construction project is perfect, you will experience ups and downs during the process. The time you spend at the beginning of your project, making connections and building trust, will pay off later. The connection you establish with your home team will enable you to calmly work through any issues that may arise. Simply put, it goes better because you're all on the same side.

The Last Word

Connect can be hard to define. It's hard to know if you're hiring the right home professionals for your team. Take your time, just as you would if you owned a company and you were hiring a new employee. Ask as many questions as you need to feel you have a good fit. Spend the time up front to keep from having disappointments later.

CHAPTER 4

COMMUNICATE

Because you've done your homework *and* your research in the previous chapter, **Connect**, you know, or have some idea, how you want your finished home project to look.

You should also know, at least roughly, what your budget is, and you've interviewed professionals about your project.

Congratulations! In so many cases, knowing what you want and finding the right team to make it happen are the hardest parts of a home renovation project!

Now that you have your team in place, we move on to the second 'C' in our 4-C process: **Communicate**.

Communicate covers:

- *Expectations.* Understanding the design process and how the homeowner fits in.

- *Teamwork.* Keeping the connection with your team open for the life of the project.

- *Planning.* Setting yourself up for success by planning ahead.

Expectations

So you've signed your contracts, and your architect, designer, and general contractor know exactly what you want. Now it's up to them to execute, stay within your proposed budget, and in a few short weeks, you'll have your dream home.

Right?

Well, not quite.

You are the homeowner, and your architect, designer, and general contractor are going to do the best they can to make you happy. However, there's no such thing as a perfect construction project. All sorts of things can, and do, go wrong, through no fault of yours—*or theirs*.

A normal demolition may reveal years of hidden structural damage or decay. Local laws may prevent you from adding an extra half bath in the basement of your house. Neighbors' concerns may limit the hours your team is able to work on your project. The list goes on.

Mission-critical to the outcome of your project is that you *manage expectations.*

Part of managing expectations is making sure that every member of the team fulfills his or her role. As a homeowner, your role is *central to the process* ... but not necessarily in charge of it.

That can be a scary concept; we'll give you a minute!

Ready?

Yes, you are about to spend a lot of money, and yes, you will have to live with the finished product, so your wants and needs should matter most. And yes, doing a renovation right can add tens of thousands of dollars in value to your home. But it's also true that doing it wrong can cost you big when it comes time to sell, so there's risk involved.

Given all that, it's normal to want to be in charge, to drive all aspects of the project.

When that feeling grips you, try to keep in mind that you've thoroughly evaluated your team's skill set, credentials, and past projects, and you've worked hard to make a connection so you can feel good about putting your trust in them.

Now is the time to do just that: *put your trust in them.*

If you hire your team, but don't give them the trust and freedom to do the work you've hired them to do, what you're really doing is undermining the success of your project.

One of the most important parts of your role as homeowner is to trust the people you've hired.

This is not to say that you should trust blindly.

Trust them to communicate with you. Know that they will tell you what you need to know and that they will answer your questions and help alleviate

Why shouldn't you, the homeowner, try to manage the job yourself? First and foremost, because you don't have any experience in the business.

And second, and don't under-estimate this one: it's a full-time job. You have to be there every day in order for your project to be completed appropriately and on time. If you're managing the project, you're essentially serving as your own general contractor, which means there's no one else to rely on when the project gets complicated, or worse, when things go wrong.

any concerns. And to make sure you have a forum to get your questions and concerns addressed, the process is set up so that you and your team will have regular contact, through which everyone's expectations can be managed.

Teamwork

So you get why teamwork is so important, but how do you start?

Begin your project by setting up a kickoff meeting with the key players on your team: your architect, your general contractor, and your designer. At this meeting, you'll go over the proposed plan, the proposed schedule, and possibly, the rough cost estimate.

You'll be asked for a lot of input here, of course, but you'll also want to listen and observe how the team members work with each other. In addition to making sure your team is crystal-clear on your wishes and desires for the project, your secondary goal here is to learn your team's communication styles—just as they are using this time to learn yours!

If you don't listen to your team's ideas, it will slow your project down.

Just because you saw two bathtubs stacked bunk-bed style (to give a very extreme example), that doesn't mean it is a good design idea, or architecturally supportable within your current structure, or even legal according to local building codes—and just because you want it, that doesn't automatically make it possible within the budget you can afford.

Your ideas are just that: ideas. Your team will also have ideas—and experience building the kinds of design you want. The more you can work with your team, the more smoothly your project will go. And it's worth noting that the more resistant you are to hearing your team's input, the more frustrated they are likely to become. Everyone on the team, the homeowner included, bears responsibility to maintain a good working relationship, to maintain your existing connection.

> *It's not always the homeowner with the wild ideas. Sometimes, designers are unrealistic because they don't know how to build, so the general contractor, the homeowner, and the designer need to work hand in hand to make sure all suggestions are realistic.*

Planning

There's a theory out there that says there are two kinds of people: the planners, and the ones who prefer to fly by the seat of their pants. If you normally like to fly without a net, this is one time you should definitely reconsider. When you're renovating or remodeling your home, having a solid, detailed plan is one of the biggest keys to homeowner happiness.

Why is that?

Any type of construction project will be like a roller coaster, and not necessarily one of the fun, little ones you'd let your kids go on.

First, you find yourself thrilled to be starting the project, full of great ideas and excitement about the way everything is going to look. You get those first architect's drawings and—well, that moment will either be a bigger high, or if the architect didn't quite put your ideas to paper the way you expected, you'll have your first low.

In any case, signing the contract usually brings you right back down to earth.

Then, you might find the demolition part of the project a ton of fun, or you might wonder exactly what the heck you've gotten yourself into—it can be unsettling to see your house broken apart. No matter how long the project takes, and even if it's progressing perfectly according to the proposed schedule, you're likely to have a moment wondering "will this project ever end?" (Maybe more than one!) You're also likely to have moments where you feel you're not in control of the process, and that's completely normal.

At some point, of course, you will see the light at the end of the tunnel, and slowly, but surely, your mood will rise, up and up until that final moment where the contractor takes every last bit of equipment and leaves you to your beautiful, newly remodeled house.

And you want to get to that happy ending as quickly as possible, don't you?

Your instinct as a homeowner is probably to speed the process along. Hurry up through the planning stages and get to the construction part, because the sooner you start construction, the sooner the job will be done, right? But in order to make your dream home a reality, you need to spend the right amount of time, up front, on *planning the job*.

The planning stage is mission-critical because that's the part of the process where you come to the table with your dreams and your budget, and the architect and contractor come to the table with their talent and years of experience, and you hammer out a design and construction plan you all can agree on.

Part of what makes the planning stage difficult is that it is in the early part of the job. You don't quite know your team yet; they don't know you that well, either. They are likely to know much more about the general construction process than you do, with a greater knowledge of what works and what doesn't. You may not have realistic ideas about the budget or how long a project will take. So there are plenty of opportunities for a communications disconnect here, and if you're not prepared to work through them, it can derail the entire process.

The trick is to keep smiling, keep talking, keep asking questions, and know that you are all working together to create a plan that makes sense for everyone on the team. After all, no contractor is going to build you a full-scale replica of the Taj Mahal for $15,000. And even if you have a bazillion dollars, you're unlikely to find a team who will be happy to build you a glass-walled two-story bathroom.

Communication as a Process

So how do you take into account all the diverging wants, needs, and opinions, and come to an agreement? Remember that it's a *process*, which means you will need multiple tries to get the plan just right. Share your ideas with your architect and listen to his or her suggestions.

Be ready to adjust your wish list, because at varying times during the job, anything and everything can change.

When you get that first set of architectural plans, look at them with an open mind. Recognize that they won't be perfect on the first try. Do your best not to get upset if your team didn't quite hit the sweet spot. (It may help to keep in mind that you're on an emotional roller coaster of sorts, and while parts of the ride can be scary or upsetting, there will be fun parts, too.)

Once you agree on a preliminary design, the next hill to climb is working through the proposed budget. Just like with that first set of drawings, the first proposed budget may cause a little "sticker shock." But remember that the proposed budget is just that: a proposal. It's the starting point for more conversation, more negotiation, and more decisions. Remember also that your contractor's goal is to please you, and that part of the process means he is ready to adjust his proposal, as best he can, to meet your needs. In the ideal case, you will also be ready to adjust your expectations accordingly.

So now you have a solid plan. You're ready! And this is why having a solid, detailed plan is so important: doing this communication work up front means you have had detailed discussions and have anticipated as many potential problems as you possibly could—before the actual work starts. You've hashed out the sticky issues in the design and the budget, which gives you three huge advantages:

- you will know immediately when the project is not progressing according to plan, and

- you're aware of any areas where, once construction has begun, you might have to deviate from the plan, and most important,

- you've come together as a team, and the group has built a relationship that will make all subsequent communications both easier and more effective.

And that's great, because the great communication you've established needs to continue throughout the process!

Almost certainly, you will encounter hidden issues that could not have been known about beforehand. For example, once construction has begun, your contractor may find more extensive water damage than was previously estimated, and fixing that, which is not optional, will require additional budget dollars and a longer schedule. Or, you may discover that a particular floor tile that was specified in the plan is no longer available in the quantities you'll need on the date you need them, and the team will have to come together and make an adjustment to the plan.

These examples are two small bumps in the road, and the road can get much rockier. Very few of these unexpected situations can actually be anticipated, which means more communication, more decisions, and more adjustments to the existing plan.

That's the *how* of great communication. Next, we'll discuss the *when*.

CHAPTER 5

CHECK OFF

So you've got your professionals hired, you've got a solid plan in place, and you've taken the time to establish good communication among the team. The next step is to make sure you're an integral part of that team. How? It's all about the Check Off, the third 'C' in our 4-C process.

Check Off covers:

- *Forum.* The best time and place to communicate with your construction professionals and how to make sure your ideas and concerns are heard.

- *Progress.* How the job progress is measured and managed throughout the project.

- *Changes.* What to do when those unexpected construction issues arise.

Forum

The most common forum to communicate with your home team takes the form of regular, weekly meetings.

Remember that at the beginning of the project, your team had the kickoff meeting for the initial discussion of the project, where all team members come together to communicate roles and requirements and make key decisions needed to plan and move the project forward. However, once the actual work starts, your contractor should hold—and you should be participating in—weekly team meetings, so that you will be kept in the loop about progress and will be there to give your opinion if any project decisions need to be made. (Don't even think about going on vacation until the construction is over!) This meeting, which is usually held at the construction site, is also your forum to express concerns or ask questions of the team.

Progress

So what happens in the weekly meeting?

TEAM TIP

Before construction starts, the architect will lead the weekly meeting. Once the project is under construction, the general contractor takes over that job. The person running the meeting also takes the meeting minutes and is responsible for distributing those minutes to all parties.

First, all key team members (architect, designer, general contractor, and homeowner) should attend the meeting. The key members may change, depending on which phase of the project you are in. At the beginning of the project, the architect, the general contractor, and the structural engineer need to be at the weekly meetings. The designer is not really needed during this time. By the middle of the project, once the architect and the structural engineer are happy with the way things are being built, the general contractor, the designer, and the homeowner will be a part of the weekly meetings.

Typically, the team will go over a project schedule much like the one on page 23. It shows what has been completed from past weeks, what will be completed during the upcoming week and upcoming month, and then, based on that data, how long the project is going to take.

The schedule checklist details what each person on the team needs to fulfill to hold up their end of the agreed-upon plan. For example, if the homeowner had a task to make the final tile selections by a certain date, then that will be one of the line items discussed as that due date nears. If you have made the decision on time, then your tile choice will be recorded and construction proceeds.

But what if you just can't make up your mind? If you miss your due date, then the team will discuss how to proceed without the information they needed—if that is even possible. In most cases, any line items that are dependent on the tile selection will need to be rescheduled downstream, which means the project will be delayed until you can make up your mind. (So you can see how important it is for you to meet the deadlines that are assigned to you by the team!)

The team reviews all schedule checklist items in this manner. This schedule review ensures that milestones are being met and any project delays are addressed.

The team will also review the completion check-off list at the weekly meeting. The check-off list consists of larger modules or sub-projects that are completed.

We usually use the project schedule as a completion check-off list, because every one of those line items must be finished in order for the project to be completed. For example, if all the plumbing work is an item on the project bid sheet, then once that line item is complete, the contractor can invoice the homeowner for that part of the project.

TEAM TIP

It is against the law for a contractor to invoice the homeowner for a portion of a project before that portion of the project is complete.

Both the schedule checklist and the completion checklist are used to monitor progress against the plan ... but construction projects rarely go perfectly according to plan. That's why you need to be prepared to handle changes!

Finally, after the meeting, your contractor should send you meeting notes or meeting minutes, as a record of what was discussed. This is just another way to keep the lines of communication clear and open and to keep everyone on the same page. If you have tasks assigned to you (say, choosing final cabinet hardware), this will be noted in the minutes.

Changes

Changes happen on almost every construction project. You could even say they are inevitable. For instance, you might come to the conclusion you don't really love

One of the best things you, as a homeowner, can do is to take lots of photographs throughout the entire process: before, during, and after. You really can't have too many photographs. These photos serve as a record of all activity on the project, but they can also be valuable as proof of the quality of the work when it comes time to sell your house. Also, photographs can prove invaluable if a problem arises with any of the work done.

the paint colors you picked, or late in the game, you might decide you'd rather have wood floors than the original terracotta tiles. These are, of course, fairly simple, straightforward changes to your original (contracted) plan.

But some changes may mean you have to go back to the drawing board—literally. For example, if you decide the back patio you're building will need to be wider by two and a half feet, and you think to yourself, "Well, it's only a couple of inches..."

It would be nice if the construction process could be that flexible, but in reality, new architectural drawings would have to be created and submitted to your city's planning department. What you may consider to be a small change may actually affect the entire process, and if you don't adjust the plan through the proper channels, your city inspector may not sign off on the project once the work is complete. Any cost or time you might have saved on the front end by trying to cut this corner will certainly come back to bite you at the end of the job.

The other key message about requesting changes is that changes must be requested in writing, never verbally. By all means, tell your contractor what you want to change—have that open communication and discussion first. Make sure every team member weighs in, because any change to the plan should ideally be a team decision.

Change Order

Once you've discussed the details of a particular change, your contractor should incorporate your instructions into a *change order*.

And turnabout is fair play here: your contractor should also submit a written change order for every change he would like to make to the original, agreed-upon plan.

This protects you against unexpected cost or schedule overruns.

Written change orders are the single best way to ensure your wishes are conveyed completely and get forwarded to all members of the team. Remember the "telephone game" you may have played in school? You'd whisper a message to the person next to you, who would tell the kid next to him, and so on, and eventually the original message would come out completely garbled on the other end of the line.

The change order describes exactly what the homeowner wants to change, what that change will cost, and how that change will affect the schedule and completion date. Most important, the change order will be signed and dated by both the homeowner and the contractor, and once signed, it becomes part of the existing contract.

The same thing can happen here. What you tell your contractor may not be perfectly described to your designer or architect, who may then change the plans in a way that still doesn't get you to the finished product you wanted. When you put your wishes in writing, there is much less chance they will be interpreted incorrectly— and this, in turn, helps preserve the good communication you've worked so hard to develop and keeps your business relationship with your home team intact.

An example of a change order is shown on the next page.

CHANGE ORDER

BUILDING A STRONG FUTURE

Name of Owner:
Project:
Address:
Date:
Change Order #:
Name:

1. Replace existing partition wall between kitchen and living room areas that were damaged by the fire.
2. Remove plaster and re-frame the wall up to code.
3. Cut back existing ceiling joist members that were damaged by the fire and reinforce them to bring them up to code and prevent any further safety hazards.
4. Replace partial kitchen sub-floor that was damaged by the fire. Re-frame sub-floor joist members and install new ¾ inch T&G plywood.
5. Remove stucco in the east corner side of house and repair and replace any framing wood members that are damaged due to termite and dry rot.
6. Install 380 square foot deck. Ipe 1" deck boards. Screwed from top with Stainless steel screws. Screws must be pre-drilled. Ends of Ipe needs to be waxed.
7. Run 2 extra circuits from basement to upstairs bedroom closet (15amp).
8. Rewire 11 outlets on second floor with one new circuit.
9. Rewire four outlets on first floor with one new circuit.
10. Ran 3/4 gas line from main meter to water heater, 20 feet. Ran 1/2 gas line from water heater to attic for furnace, 25 feet.
11. Drywall, patch, paint. 2'x7' opening in upstairs bedroom to run gas line up to attic.

Date of Existing Contract _____

Above change(s) to be performed under same terms and conditions as specified in original contract unless otherwise stipulated

_____   _____   _____
Contractor Signature   Authorized Signature   Date

In addition to change orders, there are a few other tools used to manage changes to a project.

Extra Work Order

What if you decide, after construction has started in your soon-to-be-new kitchen, that you'd like to add a pass-through in the wall? You've never even discussed the idea, but you just saw one on the DIY Channel and now you want one, too. Since this wasn't included in the original plans, your contractor will write an *extra work order*.

Remember that you agreed to the plan, just as the rest of the team did. Remember that your team can't just move a wall four feet because that makes the job easier for them … and you can't, either. If you want to make a design change after the plan has been agreed upon, you need to renegotiate that change with the team, just as they would have to do with you. The extra work order will detail the particulars of the change, as well as new budget line items, and it will also include information about how the new work will impact the existing schedule. The signed extra work order then becomes a part of your contract.

Request for Information

Another situation that happens is a *request for information*, or RFI. Sometimes, the information provided by the architect in the plan is not detailed enough for the general contractor to proceed. When this happens, the contractor may submit an RFI.

When might this happen? If the plan specifies existing 2x6 walls, and the contractor pulls away sheetrock and discovers the walls are actually 2x4, he will send an RFI to the architect so that there is agreement about how to proceed. This is more likely to happen at the beginning of the project, but it can occur at any time.

Keep in mind that it's not going to be fun when you first find out that even after all that planning, something unexpected has come up in your construction process—but just knowing unexpected things can happen may help keep you from overreacting. Remember also that your contractor doesn't want to be the bearer of bad news, but sometimes, he has to.

Let's look at another example. If the design specifies "white marble tile," the contractor may need more information about the manufacturer, size, etc., because different sizes of tile may cost more or less, may take longer to install, etc. Since each of these decisions affects the homeowner's schedule and the budgeted bottom line, the entire team must be brought into agreement before the contractor can proceed.

A sample RFI is shown below.

RFI

▶ BALI
BUILDING A STRONG FUTURE

Name of Owner:
Project:
Address:
Date:
RFI #:
Name:

_____

SIDING DETAIL

1. The 3" wood projection and galvanized flashing at the curved window head will need to be supplied and installed by others.
2. Is there any other trim on the sides or sill of these curved windows? And if so what is the detail?
3. What is the material for the wood slats and will it hold up on that curved radius?
4. How are the wood slats fastened? Needs to hold up over time and weather.
5. Please specify the Hardie smooth beaded lap you want used?
6. Is the detail to align the bead in the Hardie to the gap in the slatted siding? Meaning is this critical or not to align these elements somehow?
7. What is the siding detail on the inside of the rail above the vestibue?
8. Is there any trim on the balance of the windows and if so what is it?
9. The outside corners show no trim and you can't miter Hardie siding. Please provide detail for inside and outside corners?

BATHROOM

1. No specifications for tile around shower tub.
2. What type of wood are we using for the bathroom vanity.

Next Steps

At this point, you should understand the times and places you'll be communicating with your team about the project, as well as some of the tools your contractor will use if and when things don't go according to plan. With your dream team in place, you'll be able to handle any bump in the road. Through the good communication channels you've established, you can trust that any issues will be resolved so that everyone is happy.

Then, just about the time you're getting comfortable with all the chaos, the magic day will arrive, and it will be time to go through the completion phase of the project. That's next!

CHAPTER 6

COMPLETION

After reading the previous chapter, you now have a good understanding of how your home team will communicate with each other during the project.

So what's next? **Completion** includes:

- *Punch List.* A detailed list of all items that need to be completed.

- *Liens and Notices.* All the legal notices that are filed as the project nears completion.

- *Construction Manual.* A binder containing a description and photos of all the work done and materials used, plus warranty and care information.

Punch List

A punch list is a list of tasks that need to be done in order to complete—meet the terms of—a construction contract. They are usually generated in the final phase of construction. For example, the contractor may walk through the construction area and note any remaining issues that need to be fixed.

TEAM TIP

Once the punch list has been generated, your contractor should go over it with both you and the designer, to make everyone is on the same page with respect to the finishing items.

An example punch list is included below.

PUNCH LIST

▶ BALI
BUILDING A STRONG FUTURE

Name of Owner:
Project:
Address:
Date:
Punch List #:
Name:

BATHROOM / LAUNDRY ROOM
1. Towel Ring - over electrical plug.
2. Have medicine cabinet made. 21 1/2" wide x 30" Tall x 3" depth. Per TJ spec.
3. Install screen.
4. Install towel bar. CI will order the new towel bar.
5. Install door stop for shower door.
6. Install bathroom door stop.
7. Install shower head.
8. Caulk in back of toilet with white caulk.
9. Install door handle. CI needs to order it.
10. Install light fixture in the laundry room.
11. Caulk in back of counter top with white caulk in laundry room.
12. Install cover caps in cabinets.
13. Caulk floor tile where door is located in between laundry room / bathroom.

KITCHEN
1. Door handle for barn door. CI needs to order it.
2. Barn door stop. Per TJ spec. L bracket with floor guide.
3. Caulk brick (cement) by refrigerator.
4. Install cabinet hardware. KI and CI need to get new hardware, screws are incorrect. Hardware will eventually break.
5. Install plug for Coffee maker.
6. Install Toe kick by dishwasher.
7. Dimmer is not working next to refrigerator.
8. Caulk trim about door going into basement.
9. Install threshold in basement door.
10. Install bigger switch plates for electrical plug by basement door.

EXTERIOR
1. Install 1x4 under window with curbus.
2. Where deck landing is located sand down with gorilla glue and re-stain.

Punch lists can contain a large variety of items, depending on the type and scope of the job. Some of these items may seem on the small side, or maybe not worth worrying about, but keep in mind that your contractor is being paid to complete every aspect of the job and leave your house in clean, perfect condition.

Finally, make sure you check everything: be sure that all of the punch list items have been completed to your satisfaction before you pay your general contractor—or anyone else.

> *A punch list got its name because people used to punch a hole in the paper next to each item that had been completed.*

Liens and Notices

You might notice an increase in the amount of paperwork you see during the Completion phase. As I'm licensed in California, those are the laws and practices I'll be sharing with you in this chapter, but keep in mind that the paperwork and laws change from state to state.

Preliminary Notice

Throughout the project, subcontractors and suppliers may file *preliminary notices* (sometimes called *20-day notices* or *prelims*). This is a heads-up to the homeowner, the general contractor, the lender, the escrow company, and the bonding company that:

- there's a subcontractor out there who needs to be paid, and

- the subcontractor has lien rights.

As a homeowner, you should already have a list (from your contractor) of every subcontractor and supplier he will be using during the course of the project. So when you receive a 20-day notice, you should verify that the

subcontractor or supplier is already on your list. If not—
don't let it slide. Check with your contractor.

Mechanic's Lien

A *mechanic's lien*[*] records an interest in the title to real
property for the benefit of parties who have supplied
labor or materials, or both, to improve the property.

In very simplified terms, a mechanic's lien is a document
your general contractor, a subcontractor, or material
supplier may use to levy a claim, or "hold," against the
title of your house. It is designed to protect the general
contractor, subcontractor, or material supplier by giving
the homeowner an incentive to ensure that not only the
general contractor gets paid, but that any subcontractor
or material supplier also gets paid, once a project has
been completed. A mechanic's lien holds the homeowner
responsible for payment to any subcontractor or material
supplier, even if the general contractor has already been
paid for the services of the subcontractor or material
supplier.

Most frequently, a mechanic's lien is filed when a general
contractor fails to pay subcontractors or material
suppliers. Even though the homeowner has a signed
contract solely with the general contractor, the recording
of a mechanic's lien by a subcontractor or material
supplier holds the homeowner responsible for payment
even if the homeowner has already paid the general
contractor.

A mechanic's lien must be recorded before a contractor,
subcontractor, or material supplier can proceed to file a

---

[*] This section regarding mechanic's liens is intended only to provide the reader with a general
overview of complicated and time-sensitive legal issues. Neither the author nor any of the
contributors by way of the mechanic's lien section or otherwise intend to and are not giving
legal advice. If you have specific questions regarding mechanic's liens, construction or real
estate law, you should seek the advice of a licensed attorney.

foreclosure action to foreclose based on the mechanic's lien.

So let's go over that scenario one more time: the work was completed, and you paid the general contractor. For some unknown reason, the general contractor did not pay his subcontractors, and even though you, the homeowner, have no relationship with the subcontractors, you can be held responsible to pay them!

If a lien is filed against your property, you may end up experiencing one or all of the following:

- you may have to pay double for the same job,

- you may have a recorded lien on your property, which can affect your ability to refinance, borrow against, or even sell your home,

- you may be forced into foreclosure if you do not pay the lien.

Notice of Completion

A *notice of completion* is a formal, written notice signed by the owner of a project to notify all concerned parties that work on the project has been completed.

This document is recorded in the county where the work was completed, and a copy is sent via certified mail to the general contractor and any other companies, suppliers, or laborers who have a financial interest in the project—in other words, anyone who should have been paid by the homeowner or general contractor during the course of the project.

In California, a notice of completion must contain specific information required by code, including:

- the date of completion,

- the name and address of the owner,

- a description of the site and the street address,

- the name of the original contractor.

Remember that a notice of completion must be recorded at the office of the county recorder in the county where the construction project was located—*and* it has to be done within fifteen days after the work has been completed. Some counties allow you to file via the Internet, and as you'd expect, there is a recording fee, no matter how you file.

So what's in it for you, the homeowner, to take the time and expense to file this notice? A notice of completion protects you because it reduces the amount of time any financially interested parties (contractors, subcontractors, or material suppliers) have to record a mechanic's lien on your property.

This information has probably got your heart pounding a bit. So what can you do to protect yourself?

How to Protect Yourself

The best way to protect yourself is to ask your contractor to get lien waivers from everyone he is responsible for paying. That said, it may not be in the contractor's best interest to do this—but a reputable contractor will provide this to you.

Keep track of Preliminary Notices so you're sure you know who is working on your project and who should be getting paid.

Before you make a payment, make sure you get a signed *conditional release* from any potential lien claimants. (If you ask your general contractor for this release, he is required to give it to you.) After you pay, the contractor should give you an *unconditional release* signed by each potential claimant. Note that, by law, you may withhold future payments until you get the signed, unconditional release for the previous payment.

Remember that when we go into legal details, we're talking about California law. You can research the specifics and more about how to protect yourself at your state or county's contractor's licensing board (for example, at http://www.cslb.ca.gov/Resources/ GuidesAndPamphlets/HomeownersGuideToPreventing MechanicsLiens.pdf) and also at http://www.nolo.com.

Construction Manual

At the end of every job, I deliver to the homeowner a construction manual. Homeowners need to get a construction manual every time because there are a lot of things within a construction project that you need to have, such as appliance manuals, the types of paint, wood, and roofing you used for your project, and what types of sustainable green building products were used. This is all included in the manual that the general contractor needs to make for the homeowner, which is really important.

Warranties for materials and appliances are also very important to the homeowner, so I include them in the construction manual. Your contractor should do this for you, as well—and if he doesn't and something subsequently breaks, your first call should be back to that contractor.

Close-Out

Close-out and the final stages are the hardest parts of a construction project. It always comes down to the fine line where everyone on the team needs to work extra hard to get the project done on time.

This is the very end of your "roller-coaster ride," and you might be emotional at this point in the journey. It bears repeating that maintaining your regular communication, remembering that the contractor is trying his best to make you happy, and having a sense of humor will help you get through this phase of the project.

CHAPTER 7

RECAP AND COMMON QUESTIONS

Recap: The Four Cs

Remember, the Four Cs that will help you communicate with your general contractor, architect, and designer to get the results you want are:

- **Connect.** Do your homework, do your research, and then listen to what your prospective home team tells you about their skills and your project.

- **Communicate.** Manage your expectations, work as a team, and spend as much time as possible on up-front planning.

- **Check-Off.** Make sure to communicate within the right forum, keep track of how progress is measured on the project, and understand how changes impact the project timeline.

- **Completion.** Make use of communication tools like punch lists, understand your rights and responsibilities with respect to liens and notices, and make sure you understand the content of the construction manual and warranties your contractor provides to you.

Common Questions

Q: What is the most common mistake homeowners make with their construction projects?

A: The mistake I see most often is not investing money into the plans, the architectural plans. When you don't invest time and money into the plans, it really slows things down on the project, because there are a lot of question marks once the general contractor actually starts doing the work. That results in a lot of questions with the architect, which, while absolutely necessary, just slows the project down.

If the homeowner invested the money into the first part of the drawing stage with the architect, laid everything out, and had everything picked out as far as siding and window detail, not only will everything be organized prior to starting the construction, the act of doing the planning can definitely make the homeowner more involved in, and more excited about, the experience.

Q: What happens if you don't listen to your construction team members when they give you ideas?

A: Since each member of your team is experienced in his field, you're paying for their expertise. If you don't listen to your experts, it's going to slow the project down. This, in turn, may result in irritation for the homeowner because the project won't be finished in time.

Q: How do you manage expectations on a construction project?

A: Try to remember that nothing is ever perfect on a construction project. The more you can keep your expectations realistic, the happier you'll be throughout the process. That doesn't mean you need to keep your expectations low, just try to be realistic.

Q: What is the best way to keep construction costs down on your project?

A: Remember that change orders can happen, even on a well-planned project. But if you're the kind of person who likes to change her mind, each change is likely to add cost to the project, as well as increase the length of time needed to complete the project.

Final Take-Aways

We're here, at the close-out of the book. Let's take a minute to review, one more time, the concepts I hope are clearer now that you've read the book.

- You're familiar with the general organization of a construction project and the roles of an architect, a designer, a structural engineer, a general contractor—and, as the homeowner, you also know your own role.

- You know how to research, interview, and choose the right team *for you.*

- You have an appreciation for how important teamwork is to the process and to an outcome that will make you happy.

- You're able to communicate your wishes and desires to your construction team, and you're also ready to listen to their expert advice.

- You understand how to protect yourself and your property against title claims.

- You're comfortable trusting your team to do their very best for you.

Living through all of the phases of a construction project can be harder than you might expect. It can feel like a full-time job, and it can also feel like a wild, out-of-control roller coaster.

But just like your day job, or a roller coaster, the work involved in creating your dream home can also be fun.

Be excited to move forward with your construction project, knowing that your HOME TEAM has your back every step of the way.

ACKNOWLEDGEMENTS

My thanks to the following TEAM professionals who generously lent their time and expertise to this book:

Architects:

Tom Beckett
tBP/Architecture
1000 Burnett Avenue
Ste 320
Concord, CA 94520
Tel. (925) 246-6419
www.tbparchitecture.com

Thomas Pippin, AIA
Lifebox Studios
425 E. 11th St. #26
Oakland, CA 94606
Tel. 510-922-1547
www.lifeboxstudios.com

Craig O'Connell, AIA
COA
3150 18th Street, Mailbox 409
San Francisco, CA 94110
Tel. 415-516-8047
www.craig-oconnell.com

Structural Engineer:

Justen Peek, P.E.
DP Advanced Engineering
200 Sand Creek Road, Suite D
Brentwood, CA 94513
Tel. 925-516-3502
www.advancedengineeringinc.com

ABOUT KEVIN BALESTRIERI

Kevin Balestrieri grew up in Walnut Creek, California, and got his start in, of all places, the seafood industry! His father, Sal, owned a fish distribution business in its third generation of operations at San Francisco's famous Fisherman's Wharf. As a teen, Kevin was a talented baseball and football player, who eventually received a walk-on opportunity to play football at Oregon State University. From there, he left to play on scholarship at Cal Poly San Luis Obispo. Upon graduation from Cal Poly, he moved to San Francisco and found jobs in telephone, Internet, and television sales.

Never one to just sit around, Kevin began DJ-ing at nightclubs, which eventually led to six whirlwind years traveling and spinning tunes across the U.S., as well as Mexico, Colombia, and Spain.

One morning, he woke up wanting a new challenge and decided to become a carpenter and learn the construction business. He's not quite sure why the urge came to him—but he's very glad it did.

Kevin went through the construction management program at Hayward State University and worked in construction supply sales with his brothers, Scott and Todd, while studying for his contractor's license.

Once licensed, he began with residential construction, moved into commercial construction, and his business grew. In fact, it's still growing, with 20 employees and counting. Currently, Bali Construction does general contracting, construction management, design/build, specialty projects, and service maintenance, completing more than 100 projects a year.

Every day, he looks forward to the fun of working with homeowners and helping them make their dream home a reality.